CHICAGO
FROM ABOVE

CAMERON DAVIDSON

Text by
MAGDA NAKASSIS

MYRIAD BOOKS

CHICAGO'S JAGGED SKYLINE stands tall against the Lake Michigan shoreline. At 307 miles long and 118 miles wide, Lake Michigan is the largest lake in the country, creating the impression that the city sits on an ocean. Standing on 30 miles of sandy shoreline, Chicago's buildings appear to be in a competition to reach the sky, many of them precariously placed on the water's edge. From Lake Michigan's perspective, Chicago looks like a jumble of high-rises, but in fact the city is more than just towering offices, and includes hundreds of green parks and many world-class museums. Chicago is renowned for the unique way that its buildings' designs are directly related to their function, an architectural concept that is central to the Chicago School. The city is teeming with architectural masterpieces of various styles – ranging from the minimalist modernism of the Sears Tower to the dramatic, neo-Gothic Water Tower. As the home of the modern skyscraper, this Midwestern metropolis showcases the power and grit of urban architecture.

▶ FACING SOUTH, **BELMONT HARBOR** seems very far removed from the sea of skyscrapers. This lovely inlet is surrounded by the greenery of Lincoln Park, and provides an escape from city living. Visitors can fish for salmon and trout, sail on Lake Michigan or simply have a picnic on the lakefront.

▲ ON THE OTHER side of Lake Shore Drive is **NORTH AVENUE BEACH**, a long stretch of sand next to Lincoln Park. What appears to be a docked ocean liner is **THE NORTH AVENUE BEACH HOUSE**, a $7m project that occupies 22,000sq ft of the lakefront. Here, visitors can get a snack at the outdoor eatery, wash up at the showers or rent bikes, chairs and volleyball equipment. The beach is a hive of activity, with visitors peeking through portholes for one of the best views of Chicago, and others whizzing down the lakefront trail on rollerblades and bicycles.

◀ **LAKE SHORE DRIVE** divides Chicago's skyscrapers from the sandy shore, with eight lanes of traffic that accommodate roughly 35,000 drivers every day. Lake Shore Drive's property has been up-scale and fashionable ever since entrepreneur Potter Palmer built his lavish home here in 1882. At that time, there were nearly 200 millionaires living in Chicago, all of whom flocked to Lake Shore Drive and gave rise to its all too appropriate nickname, "the **GOLD COAST**." These desirable addresses come with price tags to match – and remain popular despite the fact that they are built on swampland and landfill. The old money mansions have been replaced with glass and steel high-rises, but the extra stories provide stunning views of Lake Michigan. Four single-family homes remain on Lake Shore Drive, dwarfed by the tall white skyscraper to their left.

▲ TRAVELLING SOUTH along the coast, Lake Shore Drive curves round Lake Michigan, creating a distinctive corner of property. Perpendicular to Lake Shore Drive is an exclusive tree-lined street, **EAST LAKE SHORE DRIVE**, a row of eight historic buildings. They were all designed by the same architectural firms between 1910 and 1929, creating a unified, elegant front that imitates the grand Parisian buildings of the same era. At the far end is the luxurious Drake Hotel, followed by "The Drake Tower," "The Mayfair," "The Breakers," and four other residential high-rises. These luxurious apartments are at the highest end of the real estate market, as they stand just next to "The Magnificent Mile" and are surrounded by "the Gold Coast." The penthouse of "The Breakers," for example, sold for just under $5m in 2000.

▲ STANDING JUST left of center, **860-880 LAKE SHORE DRIVE** is perhaps the most famous address in Chicago, as well as a staple of 20th-century architecture. These twin 26-story towers, with their perfect proportions and "skin and bone" structure, are the perfect example of Chicago's International Style. Designed by German architect Ludwig Mies van der Rohe, they were built between 1949 and 1951, and immediately nicknamed the "glass houses." Mies, director of the Bauhaus school of design during the 1930s, single-handedly brought European modernism to the United States – and his architectural legacy is visible throughout the Chicago skyline.

▶ THE LAKEFRONT wall of skyscrapers is broken by **LAKE SHORE PARK**, a narrow stretch of green that gives Chicago residents a brief glimpse of natural beauty. The park is flanked by luxury residential high-rises with pricey views of Lake Michigan and Lake Shore Park. At the far end of the park is the **MUSEUM OF CONTEMPORARY ART**, a sleek building that houses works by Marcel Duchamp, Andy Warhol and Alexander Calder. Beyond is the **WATER TOWER**, a Chicago landmark that is unfortunately overshadowed by the lanky **PARK HYATT CHICAGO HOTEL** standing just beyond, and the **WATER TOWER PLACE** skyscraper to its right. The old Water Tower is one of two public buildings that survived the Great Chicago Fire of 1871, which burned for 36 hours straight. With its Gothic Revival-style architecture, the Water Tower stands out – though Oscar Wilde described it as a "monstrosity with pepper boxes stuck all over it."

▲ THE WHITE MARBLE-CLAD tower in the foreground is the **AON CENTER**, also known as the Amoco Building. On the right is **MARINA CITY**, two bizarre, battery-shaped buildings. Better known to locals as "the corn cobs," Marina City is a tribute to Midwestern agriculture, as well as a reminder that Chicago has always been at the vanguard of modern architecture. The twin 60-floor cylinders were designed as a city within a city, complete with their own apartments, markets, restaurants and 18 floors of parking space. To their right is the sleek, black **IBM BUILDING**, an excellent example of Ludwig Mies van der Rohe's minimalist architecture.

◄ THE **CNA PLAZA** stands apart from the South Michigan "streetwall" thanks to its bright red exterior. In front, on the right, is the **STRAUS BUILDING**, a neoclassical building whose crowning ziggurat is seen here at a dramatic angle.

▶ FACING THE mountainous black Sears Tower from Grant Park, several famous buildings pop up from the downtown core. On the left is the white terracotta **RAILWAY EXCHANGE BUILDING**, better known as the "Santa Fe Building." Designed by Daniel Burnham, the building now appropriately houses the Chicago Architecture Foundation. Just in front of the Sears Tower, on the left, the **CHICAGO BOARD OF TRADE** soars above the other skyscrapers. Its exterior has a geometric art deco design. To its right is **190 SOUTH LASALLE STREET**, a high-rise with curiously old-fashioned gabled windows. This charming postmodern skyscraper contains Anthony Caro's 28ft-bronze sculpture, "Chicago Fugue," an ornate tapestry of Burnham's 1909 Chicago Plan and a lobby with a 55ft-vaulted, gold leaf ceiling.

▲ ON THE EDGE of the Gold Coast, Lake Shore Drive curves around Oak Street Beach – a fashionable place for city slickers to sunbathe during summer. Just behind this sandy spot are several famous buildings, including **THE DRAKE HOTEL**, "a symbol of white glove elegance" since 1920. Appearing squat in front of the towering skyscrapers, the 12-story hotel stands out with its red neon sign. With its brilliant chandeliers and opulent red carpets, the Drake is the first choice for most visiting celebrities. Standing just behind the Drake is the **PALMOLIVE BUILDING**, whose 37 floors dominated the North Side's skyline when it was built in 1927. The art deco skyscraper was built for Palmolive soap manufacturers, but became known as the "Playboy Building" in 1965 when it became the magazine's headquarters. But in 1970, the **JOHN HANCOCK CENTER**

overshadowed everything. At 1,127ft and occupying 1.1m sq ft, the building is simply mammoth. The observatory on the 94th floor is open to the public, and visitors can sip on cocktails at the Signature Bar, which overlooks the city from a height of over 1,000 ft. The gleam of red and yellow lights beyond outline North Michigan Avenue, better known as "The Magnificent Mile."

▶ THE CORE OF downtown Chicago is known as "The Loop," nicknamed after the elevated train track that encircles the area. To the right is **BANK ONE PLAZA**, which stands out with its flared bellbottom design. But the **SEARS TOWER**, above all else, stands out in the crowd of skyscrapers. The tallest building in North America, it is 1,454ft tall and weighs 225,000 tons.

GRANT PARK is known as Chicago's "front yard," a long green expanse that spans Chicago Harbor. Built over the debris from the 1871 fire, the park features a playground, sculpture park, promenade and beautifully manicured gardens. The grounds have been landscaped in the Renaissance style of Louis XIV's Versailles, with their symmetrical design and stately promenades. The park's centerpiece, BUCKINGHAM FOUNTAIN, is also modeled on Versailles' Latona Basin, though Chicago's version is twice as big. The spring of its 133 water jets, which reach a height of 150ft, marks the beginning of summer. Though skyscrapers surround it, the park's only building is the low-lying ART INSTITUTE OF CHICAGO, built in 1893 for the World's Fair. Amongst its collection of 30,000 works are Grant Wood's *American Gothic* and van Gogh's *Self-Portrait*.

◄ THE BUILDINGS THAT line the border of Grant Park are varied in size, shape and architectural style. On the far right, with its distinctive diamond-shaped roof, is the **SMURFIT-STONE BUILDING**. As the top of the skyscraper faces the lake, this building is often said to resemble a boat. Its angled, diamond roof is lined with white light bulbs, which are replaced with colored bulbs on holidays. To its left, standing low and wide, is the **CHICAGO CULTURAL CENTER**. As the "People's Palace," the Cultural Center has always been the mayor's choice for welcoming presidents, royalty and diplomats, as well as Chicago's main venue for the performing arts. Built in the beaux-arts style of architecture, the building contains rooms based on the Doge's Palace in Venice and the Acropolis in Athens. Still further left is the **UNIVERSITY CLUB OF CHICAGO**, easily identified with its slanting roof and neo-Gothic spires. This exclusive club still maintains several traditional policies, including a dress code and strict membership requirements.

▼ ON THE SOUTH SIDE of Grant Park is **SOLDIER FIELD**, home of the Chicago Bears. Built in the 1920s during the "Golden Age of Sports," the stadium is modeled on the arenas of ancient Greece, with Doric colonnades that rise 100ft above the playing field. This grand stadium seats 66,950, contains 575,000sq ft of metal decking, 270,000sq ft of carpeting, and uses 1.25 m watts of power to illuminate the field.

On the bank of Lake Michigan stands the **MUSEUM CAMPUS**, a 57-acre park that contains Chicago's main educational attractions, connected by walkways through landscaped gardens and large patches of green. Between the three institutions, the Museum Campus draws approximately four million visitors annually. On the lakefront's edge stands the **ADLER PLANETARIUM AND ASTRONOMY MUSEUM** (left), where visitors can travel through space and time with virtual-reality technology, go to the Milky Way on a computer-animated 3-D trip and watch the stars come to life in its original domed theater. **THE FIELD MUSEUM** (top) is one of the finest natural history collections in the world, holding over 20m cultural and scientific objects. Most famously, it is the home of "Sue," the world's largest and most complete Tyrannosaurus Rex fossil, revived after 67m years inside the earth. Since it opened its doors in 1929, the **JOHN G. SHEDD AQUARIUM** (right) has delighted children and adults with its underwater population of beluga whales, rockhopper penguins, bonnethead sharks and 650 other species of aquatic animals.

THE **CHICAGO HARBOR BREAKWATER LIGHT** was first lit in 1893, and is still in operation. Floating in the middle of Lake Michigan is a 48ft-steel tower, foghorn and boathouse. Its 10-sided lantern and its powerful red flashes of light played a large role in the development of Chicago's port. At the confluence of the Chicago River and Lake Michigan sits **NAVY PIER**, a 3,000ft-long amusement park jutting out from Chicago's North Side. Originally a shipping wharf, Navy Pier has gone on to serve many purposes since its construction in 1914. During World War I, the pier housed military regiments and Red Cross units, and during the 1940s, 15,000 pilots were trained and qualified here, including the future 41st president, George Bush. Decades later, Navy Pier was revamped as an ultra-modern family entertainment center that includes a 150ft-Ferris wheel, antique carousel, miniature golf course, IMAX theater, and countless shops and restaurants. The Navy Pier also hosts a variety of music concerts, business conferences and trade shows at its Skyline Stage and Festival Hall – as well as an unforgettable Fourth of July fireworks display over Lake Michigan. Hundreds of millions of dollars have gone into the maintenance and renovation of the historic landmark, successfully attracting eight million visitors annually, and making it Chicago's number one tourist destination.

THE **CHICAGO RIVER** is the Windy City's lifeline, its original highway and the main reason that pioneers settled upon this wild spot of land over 200 years ago. The Chicago River connects the Great Lakes to the Mississippi River, making it the cultural and industrial hub of America's heartland. Since Chicago was founded, the river has undergone massive changes and suffered the tragic environmental consequences of industrialization. It has been dredged, straightened, deepened – and quite dramatically, in 1900, engineers reversed the Chicago River's direction to flow out of Lake Michigan.

▲ FACING UPSTREAM across Lake Shore Drive, the Chicago River runs through the city center. Historically, the riverside was flanked by factories for the meat packing and timber industries, but the cityscape has since changed. The tallest building in the foreground is the **AON CENTER**, formerly known as the Standard Oil Building or "Big Stan." Beyond it stands the Sears Tower, looming large and ominous in the background, as always. When the Sears Tower was erected in 1974, it replaced "Big Stan" as Chicago's tallest skyscraper.

▶ THE **EISENHOWER EXPRESSWAY** travels over the South Branch of the Chicago River, and through the **U.S. POST OFFICE BUILDING**. This art deco building was the largest post office in the world when it was built in 1932.

◀ FACING DOWNSTREAM toward the lake, the trapezoidal **MERCHANDISE MART** sits where the Chicago River splits into its North and South Branches. This immense building was built during the business boom of the 1920s, in order to centralize the city's wholesale goods trade. In 1945, Joseph P. Kennedy purchased the building for a hefty $16m, and it stayed in the family until the 1990s. Merchandise Mart sprawls over two city blocks, containing the Chicago Transit Authority headquarters, an "L" train station and endless showrooms. Every year, over three million visitors come to see the world's largest commercial center, which is also the second largest building of any kind, next to the Pentagon.

▶ NEAR THE MOUTH of the Chicago River is **THE WRIGLEY BUILDING**, seen here on the left. This white terracotta skyscraper is the headquarters for Wrigley chewing gum, and one of the most attractive buildings in all of Chicago. Its four-faced clock, which is two stories tall and which has a diameter of 19ft 7in, ensures that every shopper on "The Magnificent Mile" knows the time. At night, the Wrigley Building is flooded with lights, separating itself from the rest of the Chicago skyline. Its architectural blueprint follows the Seville Cathedral's Giralda Tower, but its decorative design stems from the French Renaissance style. The result is an ornate, eye-catching building that stands out next to the austere International Style buildings, such as the John Hancock Center and the Sears Tower.

IN 1922, the Chicago Tribune held an international design competition for "the most beautiful office building in the world." The result is the **TRIBUNE TOWER**, a steel skyscraper cloaked in a neo-Gothic style. The tower's gargoyle sculptures and flying buttresses imitate Rouen Cathedral, in France. Its walls are studded with stones from famous sites around the world and beyond – including fragments of Westminster Abbey, the Taj Mahal, the Parthenon and even a piece of the moon!

Peter Adams photolibrary.com

▲ HOME OF THE Chicago White Sox, **U.S. CELLULAR FIELD** is located on Chicago's South Side. In 1989, this baseball diamond replaced the aging Comiskey Park, just across the road. With a capacity of over 45,000, the high tech U.S. Cellular Field cost $167m.

▲ **NORTHWESTERN UNIVERSITY** occupies 240 acres of stunning lakefront property just north of Chicago. Founded as a private university in 1851, the institution was meant to educate the Northwest Territory, which would later become five sweeping Midwestern states. Today, Northwestern is a very prestigious university (and the runt of the Big Ten Athletic Conference), situated in the charming college town of Evanston, Illinois.

▶ OVERLOOKING THE Columbia Basin is the **MUSEUM OF SCIENCE AND INDUSTRY**, a neoclassical building devoted to the wonders of technology. The museum is largely the work of Julius Rosenwald, chairman of Sears Roebuck & Co., who visited Munich's Deutsches Museum in 1911 and was inspired to create a similar place in America for "industrial enlightenment." It is the oldest science museum in the Western hemisphere, and brings in two million visitors a year. Its exhibits are mostly interactive and focus on the 20th century, which attracts many curious children. Visitors can walk through a 16ft model of the human heart, climb aboard the revolutionary Silver Streak train and travel to Old Ben #17, a reproduction of an early Illinois coalmine.

▲ **GRACELAND CEMETERY** is the final resting place for Chicago's finest. Anyone with an interest in the city's history and architecture is compelled to come here, the famous burial ground of the Getty family, retailer Marshall Field, industrialist George Pullman, architects Daniel Burnham and Ludwig Mies van der Rohe, and many others. Its beautifully landscaped grounds are filled with various eye-catching graves, ranging from modern sculptures to ancient Egyptian pyramids and elaborate mausoleums.

▶ ON THE OUTSKIRTS of the city is the **BAHÁ'Í HOUSE OF WORSHIP**, whose pearly white dome beams against Chicago's steely landscape. "A taste of the East in the Midwest," it is the only Bahá'í house in North America, home to a faith based on the teachings of 19th-century Persian prophets. More than five million people have come here to celebrate the Bahá'í faith and to admire its stunning architecture. The building is adorned with lace-like filigree, and its sensational dome rises 135ft in the air. According to Bahá'í provisions, the house of worship has nine sides, each with an entrance and alcove, engraved with quotations from the prophet Bahá'u'lláh.

LINCOLN PARK is as much a part of Chicago as the Sears Tower or any modern skyscraper. Occupying 1,208 green acres and stretching along six miles of lakeshore beach, it is the largest urban park in the United States and the most spectacular of Chicago's 552 parks. There is something for everyone here – from cross-country skiing to bird-watching to beach-bumming. The park's recreational facilities are unbelievable, with a range of tennis courts, baseball diamonds, playing fields and even an archery range. On the **SOUTH POND** (above), landlubbers can rent paddleboats, fish for carp or sip a cold beer in the leafy shade outside **CAFÉ BRAUER**. This Chicago landmark sits at the narrow end of the pond, offering beautiful views of the park, Lake Michigan and the Chicago skyline. The restaurant is a wonderful example of the Prairie School of Architecture, a style that originated in Chicago with architect Frank Lloyd Wright, and which emphasizes a building's connection to its natural environment. Lincoln Park also contains the country's oldest public zoo, which began in 1868 when New York City donated two swans. Since then, **LINCOLN PARK ZOO** has grown considerably, now housing over 1,000 animals, including a frozen pool of polar bears and rare Siberian tigers. The zoo specializes in wildlife conservation, and uses educational exhibits to raise awareness about endangered species and environmental causes. **THE McCORMICK BIRD HOUSE** (right) contains a total of 10 different habitats that simulate the coastlands, grassy plains and tropical jungles that suit its many feathered friends. **THE LINCOLN PARK**

CONSERVATORY (left) houses a stunning collection of exotic plants under a soaring glass dome. Three acres of indoor garden give Chicago locals the pleasure of walking among delicate orchids and giant palm trees during the frozen winter months. In front of the conservatory is a broad French garden and fountain, which has become a very popular spot for picnickers.

◀ ON CHICAGO'S SOUTH SIDE is the **UNIVERSITY OF CHICAGO**, an academic institution of the highest caliber. In 1890, million dollar mogul John D. Rockefeller founded the university, later describing it as "the best investment I ever made." The university has always been a pioneer in American academic life; by 1892, it accepted both male and female, and black and white students – an extremely rare situation at the time. Its students and faculty have included 75 Nobel Prize-winners, 13 MacArthur fellowship recipients (also known as "genius grants"), two Pulitzer Prize winners and numerous Rhodes scholars. These extraordinary brains teach and learn on a faux English Gothic campus, complete with towers, spires and hideous gargoyles.

▶ HERE ON the straight streets of the Chicago suburbs, winter arrives early and stays late. The average annual snowfall is over three feet.

TWO FINAL IMAGES that capture the spirit of Chicago are **WRIGLEY FIELD** and the trains that have made Chicago the nation's "railroad capital." Home of the beloved Chicago Cubs and America's favorite pastime, Wrigley Field is the oldest National League ballpark. Other stadiums may claim larger scoreboards or newer technology – but Wrigley Field has seen it all. This is where Babe Ruth "called shot" in the 1932 World Series, where Pete Rose slammed the 4,191st hit of his career and where Gabby Hartnett hit his legendary "Homer in the Gloamin'". The network of railway tracks in and around Chicago have made it the United States' transportation hub. Historically the center of grain, cattle and industry in the Midwest – the efficiency of its trains brought jobs (and millions seeking work) to Chicago. Today, millions of passengers and countless tons of cargo are transported each and every day via Chicago's excellent transit system.

First published in 2004 by Myriad Books Limited
35 Bishopsthorpe Road, London SE26 4PA

Photographs copyright © Cameron Davidson
Text copyright © Magda Nakassis

ISBN 0 681642 45 9

Designed by Jerry Goldie

Printed in China